Cord-Cutting for Freedom

The Unique Energy Practice to Cut Off

What Sucks Your Power and

Help You Regain Your Life

PUBLISHED BY: Konstantia Karletsa

Konstantia Karletsa

Cord-Cutting for Freedom

Contents

Introduction / Writer's Letter

In the intricate tapestry of human relationships, we often find ourselves intertwined with the energies of others. Whether through deep connections with loved ones, casual acquaintances, or even fleeting interactions, our energetic fields resonate and interact in ways that can be both enriching and draining. While we naturally share our energy with those around us, we may also unknowingly become susceptible to energy leaks—those subtle, yet profound, pulls on our vitality that can leave us feeling depleted or overwhelmed.

This book explores the concept of energetic cords—those invisible threads that connect us to others. These cords can be positive, fostering love and support, but they can also become burdensome, tethering us to negative emotions, unspoken obligations, or unresolved conflicts. Understanding how these connections form and how they impact our well-being is essential for anyone seeking to cultivate a more balanced, vibrant life.

In our fast-paced world, where emotional exchanges can occur with surprising intensity, it's easy to overlook the significance of these energetic ties. We may absorb the fears, anxieties, and stresses of others, often without realizing it, leaving us vulnerable to emotional fatigue and confusion. By learning to recognize and consciously cut these cords, we empower ourselves to reclaim our energy and foster healthier, more fulfilling relationships.

Cord cutting helped me survive in difficult times and reclaim my energy. This experience made me decide to write this book. Throughout it, we will delve into the nature of energetic cords, exploring their origins, manifestations, and the ways they can affect our mental, emotional, and physical well-being. You will discover practical techniques for identifying these connections and effective methods for cutting or transforming them. From visualization exercises to grounding practices, each chapter offers tools to help you reclaim your energy and restore your sense of self.

As we embark on this journey together, remember that cutting energetic cords is not about severing ties with those we care about. Rather, it is about fostering clarity and mutual respect, creating boundaries that allow for genuine connections without the burden of unwanted energy exchanges. By embracing this practice, you will not only enhance your personal vitality but also contribute to a healthier energetic landscape for those around you.

Join me as we explore the transformative power of cutting energetic cords, reclaiming our energy, and nurturing the vibrant connections that truly nourish our souls. Together, we will embark on a path toward empowerment, healing, and profound self-discovery.

Emotions, Thoughts, and Energy

At its core, energy is the fundamental force that powers every aspect of our existence. In the physical world, energy manifests in various forms—kinetic, potential, thermal, and more. In the context of our bodies, minds, and emotions, energy takes on a more nuanced meaning, influencing our health, well-being, and interactions with the world. Energy is essential for everything we do on any level.

Our bodies are intricate systems that require energy to function optimally. This energy primarily comes from the food we consume and supports everything from muscle contraction to cellular repair.

On a more holistic level, practices such as yoga, tai chi, and even everyday activities like walking can enhance our physical energy flow. These practices encourage the circulation of energy throughout the body, promoting balance and vitality. When we engage in regular physical activity, we boost our metabolism, which helps to keep our energy levels stable and enhances our overall health.

Our thoughts are powerful energy sources that shape our reality. Neuroscience has shown that the brain operates using electrical impulses, with thoughts and emotions generating specific neural patterns. Positive thoughts can stimulate the release of neurotransmitters like dopamine and serotonin, which contribute to feelings of happiness and well-being. Conversely, negative thoughts can drain our mental energy and lead to feelings of anxiety and stress. Mindfulness and meditation practices can help rewire our thought patterns, allowing us to harness our mental energy more effectively. By cultivating awareness and focusing on the present moment, we can enhance our cognitive clarity and emotional resilience.

Emotions are another crucial aspect of our energy system. They are often seen as energy in motion—"e-motion." Each emotion carries a unique vibrational frequency. For instance, joy and love resonate at higher frequencies, while anger and fear vibrate at lower frequencies.

Being aware of our emotional energy allows us to navigate our experiences more effectively. When we acknowledge and process our emotions, we prevent them from stagnating and causing internal conflict. Techniques such as journaling, expressive arts, or talking to a trusted friend can help release pent-up emotions and restore balance.

The interplay between body, mind, and emotions creates a dynamic energy system. When one area is out of balance, it can affect the others. For example, physical stress from lack of exercise can lead to mental fatigue, while unresolved emotional issues can manifest as physical ailments.

Thoughts and feelings are intricately linked. Thoughts are the mental processes that allow us to interpret and understand our experiences, while feelings are our emotional responses to those interpretations. For instance, if we think about a past failure, it may trigger feelings of sadness or anxiety. Conversely, positive thoughts about our future can evoke excitement and hope.

Our habitual thoughts can create cognitive patterns that influence how we perceive the world. For example, a person with a tendency to think negatively might constantly see challenges as insurmountable, which can lead to a cycle of despair. In contrast, someone with a more positive outlook may view obstacles as opportunities for growth.

On the other hand, our emotions can also shape our thoughts. When we feel stressed or overwhelmed, our thinking can become clouded, leading to irrational conclusions. Developing emotional regulation skills can help us respond more thoughtfully and maintain a clearer perspective.

Thoughts and feelings directly impact our behavior. If we feel confident, we are more likely to take risks and seize opportunities. However, if we are overwhelmed by self-doubt, we might avoid situations that could lead to personal growth.

Holistic practices that integrate physical, mental, and emotional wellness, such as yoga, meditation, or even simple breathing exercises, can harmonize this energy system. These practices encourage a flow of energy that promotes health, clarity, and emotional stability.

Energy is the lifeblood of our existence, intricately woven into the fabric of our bodies, minds, and emotions. By understanding and harnessing this energy, we can cultivate a more vibrant and balanced life. Through conscious practices and self-awareness, we can transform our energy, leading to greater well-being and a deeper connection with ourselves and the world around us. Guarding our energy from people or situations that may try to harness it is vital and we will learn here techniques to both protect and recall our personal energy.

Energetic Hygiene and the Cords

Psychic hygiene is a spiritual technique to clear and cleanse your aura. Your auric field is the energy that surrounds your body. Over time we can accumulate psychic debris that can feel like an energy heaviness. This is the consequence of living in our current times. These techniques and practices can alleviate the feeling of overwhelm, frustration, and confusion. It's common to feel overloaded and like life is chaotic when our energy fields are not clear and when we are loaded down with burdens on our physical bodies.

Some simple practices of psychic clearing and aura repair, can be done daily, weekly monthly, or even seasonally. You might even do some of these practices unconsciously because they make you feel better. One practice might be taking a shower at the end of your working day. You might feel as though you need to wash off the challenges of the day. This is psychic hygiene. You might wear different clothes to work than you do at home, this can also be a form of psychic hygiene.

Energetic cords, also called energy cords, etheric cords, or spiritual cords, are invisible channels of energy that form connections between individuals, places, objects, or even past experiences. These cords serve as pathways through which emotional, mental, and spiritual energy flows, often beyond our conscious awareness.

They are created through emotional and energetic exchanges that occur in various kinds of relationships and interactions. Anytime we engage with someone on an emotional level, whether through love, conflict, or any intense emotional experience, a cord may be created. These cords can form instantly in some cases or gradually over time in others. Some thin cords may dissolve through time by themselves when a relationship is over and there is no interest or thought or emotion to feed them but many can stay and drain us even without knowing it.

Energetic cords can significantly affect our emotional, mental, and physical well-being. Cords formed from haunted pasts, psychic vampires, or attachments can drain your energy, cloud your judgment, and create emotional blockages. They act as invisible ties, linking us to people, situations, or emotions that no longer support our highest good.

However, recognizing these cords and engaging in cord-cutting practices gives us the power to reclaim our energy and restore our balance. Cutting these energetic cords isn't about severing all connections but rather releasing the unhealthy, draining attachments that are keeping us trapped. Through cord-cutting, we create space for healthier, more balanced energy exchanges and emotional freedom. This is the basis for a happier and more independent way of life.

Energetic cords can be typically formed by

1. Emotional Interactions:

The strongest cords are often created through deep emotional exchanges. Whether it's through love, anger, fear, or grief, any intense emotion shared between people has the potential to establish an energetic cord. For example, if you have a heartfelt conversation with a close friend, an energetic connection is formed. Similarly, a heated argument or unresolved conflict can also result in a cord being created, binding both parties energetically until the issue is resolved or the cord is consciously cut.

2. Repetitive Interactions:

Cords can also form through repetitive interactions, even if they are not emotionally charged. Daily interactions with family, friends, coworkers, or romantic partners often create subtle energy bonds. The more frequently we interact with someone, the stronger the cord becomes. Over time, these cords can build layers of energy based on the consistency and nature of the interactions, whether they are positive or negative.

3. Intimate or Sexual Relationships:

Sexual and intimate encounters, due to their deeply personal and vulnerable nature, create some of the strongest energetic cords. These cords can last long after a relationship has ended, particularly if there are lingering emotional attachments or unresolved issues. Sexual energy is highly potent, so even brief encounters may result in cords being established that require conscious effort to release.

4. Significant Life Events:

Energetic cords can also form in moments of heightened intensity, such as traumatic events, life-altering decisions, or major transitions. These events often involve deep emotional processing, which can create cords not only with people involved in the event but also with the memory or experience itself. For instance, someone who has experienced a significant trauma may have a cord connected to the event, which continues to affect them energetically until it is healed or released.

5. Family and Ancestral Connections:

Family relationships, especially between parents and children, carry natural energetic cords from birth. These cords form as part of the deep, primal bond that exists within families. Over time, however, these cords can become complicated, reflecting both the nurturing aspects and any unresolved family dynamics, such as feelings of guilt, obligation, or emotional wounds passed down through generations.

6. Past Relationships:

Energetic cords can linger long after a relationship ends, especially if there was a strong emotional connection. Ex-

14

partners, friends we've drifted apart from, or anyone with whom we shared a meaningful connection may still have energetic ties to us. These cords can drain energy or prevent emotional closure until they are addressed, either through personal healing or a cord-cutting practice or both of these ways for better results.

7. Attachments to Places or Objects:

It's not just people who create energetic cords—certain places, objects, or even memories can establish energetic ties. For example, a home where significant emotional events took place, or an object that holds sentimental value, can create cords that tie us to that specific energy. Sometimes we can feel emotionally tethered to a location, even if we haven't visited it in years, because of the energy we've left behind or received while there.

How do we create the cords?

The creation of energetic cords is deeply linked to the vibrational frequency of both parties involved. When two individuals interact, their energy fields (or auras) come into contact, often merging or influencing one another. If the frequency is aligned, such as in positive relationships, the cord will facilitate a healthy flow of energy. If the energy is discordant, such as in conflicts, the cord may allow for the exchange of negative energy or imbalances, contributing to stress, emotional fatigue, or conflict.

• Sympathetic Resonance:

Energetic cords are often created when there is sympathetic resonance, a phenomenon where two individuals' energy fields resonate with each other. This can happen when people share similar emotions, thoughts, or vibrations, drawing them closer energetically. This resonance strengthens the connection between them, solidifying the energetic cord.

• Unconscious Cord Creation:

Most of the time, energetic cords form unconsciously. We are often unaware of how our interactions leave energetic imprints. For example, after meeting someone for the first time, you might feel deeply connected or drained by the interaction. This can be a sign that an energetic cord was established without your awareness.

• Intention and Focus:

Energetic cords can also form through the power of intention and focus. Thinking intensely about someone, especially with strong emotion (whether positive or negative), can create a cord. This is why it's possible to feel energetically tethered to someone, even if you haven't spoken in years—your thoughts and feelings alone can sustain the cord.

How energetic cords affect us

Once formed, these energetic cords allow for a continual exchange of energy between the individuals or objects involved. This can either nourish or deplete one's energy, depending on the nature of the relationship and the energy being exchanged.

• Positive Cords:

Positive energetic cords, like those formed in loving, supportive relationships, can provide feelings of connection, security, and emotional well-being. These cords help share positive energy, providing mutual emotional and spiritual support. The flow of energy is balanced and harmonious, enhancing personal growth and happiness.

• Negative Cords:

On the other hand, cords that form from negative or toxic relationships, unresolved emotions, or traumatic events can lead to energy depletion. These cords can cause emotional blockages, anxiety, stress, or even physical discomfort. A person may feel energetically drained, restless, or burdened without understanding why because the cord allows for the continual transfer of harmful emotions or energy from one party to another.

Maintaining energetic hygiene is essential for our well-being, which includes regularly assessing and releasing cords that no longer serve us.

Life is change. As we grow and evolve things change around us. People leave us and new relationships form. We move to a new house or another country and the whole environment is changed. What is now is not necessarily what will be tomorrow. Although people usually don't like change, many times we have to adapt to new situations like a new job. Sometimes it's a new lover that we put into our lives or a break-up that leaves us struggling in pain. Whether we like change or not, we should every now and then maintain an energetic hygiene. As we take care of our bodies, cleaning and caressing them, we should take care of our energetic essence also. There are many ways to gain balance and a healthy well-being and one of them is to cut the energetic cords that no longer serve us.

Not all cords are harmful, as we have already said, but it is good to scan our energy body periodically, follow the cords to find out where each one leads, and who or what they tie you with, and cut the cords that steal our energy and vitality. Some cords are thin while others are large and thick. I will give you visualization techniques on how to scan and find your cords and then cut off the ones that either are damaging or you no longer need.

But what are the most well-known factors or situations that drain our energy?

Konstantia Karletsa

Haunted Pasts, Psychic Vampires, and the Trap of Attachment

As we grow, learn, and evolve, we will eventually have to necessarily let go of what no longer serves us. When we let go, we create space for new potential and new possibilities. Change is a basic law of nature.

Relationships are crucial for human well-being as they fulfill our fundamental need for connection, providing essential emotional support and fostering personal growth. Through others, we learn and discover more about ourselves.

Neurobiology says that positive relationships trigger the activation of reward centers in the brain and create a sense of fulfillment and happiness. On the other hand, not all relationships are healthy for us. Experiences of social rejection can induce stress responses, underscoring the profound impact relationships have on our mental and emotional states. The intricate interplay between our personal and social connections and neurobiology highlights the importance of cultivating positive relationships. But can we always keep the best for us and protect ourselves from harmful interactions?

In the realm of energy work, certain phenomena can greatly influence our emotional and energetic well-being.

Some of the most common and draining issues stem from being energetically tied to the haunted past, entangled with psychic vampires, or trapped in a cycle of attachment. These energetic dynamics often involve unhealthy cords that bind us to people, events, or emotional patterns, keeping us stuck in cycles of fear, exhaustion, or emotional overwhelm.

Understanding these concepts helps us become aware of how certain energetic attachments may be negatively affecting us—and why cutting these energetic cords is crucial for reclaiming our personal power and emotional freedom.

The Haunted Past: Energetic Imprints from Trauma

The haunted past refers to unresolved traumas, painful memories, or emotional wounds that continue to affect us long after the actual event has passed. These experiences leave energetic imprints, often in the form of cords that keep us tethered to the pain and emotions associated with that moment in time.

Even when we consciously try to move forward, the energy of these past experiences can linger, weighing us down and influencing our thoughts, emotions, and decisions. This may manifest as:

• Recurring emotional triggers tied to past events.

• A sense of feeling "stuck" in life, unable to move forward despite trying.

• Continuous thought loops or obsessive thinking about past mistakes, relationships, or traumatic experiences.

These manifestations can be seen as cords that are often attached to our energy centers (chakras), particularly the solar plexus (personal power), heart (emotions and relationships), and sacral (creativity and intimacy).

To break free from the haunted past you will have first to acknowledge the lingering emotional charge tied to the past. Releasing the past with forgiveness, first to yourself and then to others connected with these specific past events, can help dissolve the cords of pain, freeing you from the emotional burdens that are holding you back. Releasing these cords using visualization doesn't erase the past, but it does free your energy from the ongoing impact of those experiences. This is a basic example of active meditation to resolve haunted past through cord-cutting. More on this and further details will come later in the book.

Haunted Past Cord-Cutting Meditation

Visualize the situation or trauma from your past that continues to haunt you. Imagine any cords attached to it, likely connecting to your heart or solar plexus. Using a golden light sword, gently cut the cords while mentally repeating an affirmation such as: "I release the past, and I am free to move forward with peace." Watch the cords dissolve into light as you feel the emotional weight lifting.

Psychic Vampires: Energy Drain through Unhealthy Attachments

The term psychic vampire refers to individuals who, often unknowingly, drain others of their energy. These people may come into our lives as close friends, family members, coworkers, or romantic partners. The energetic cords that form between you and a psychic vampire can be deeply draining, leaving you feeling exhausted, anxious, or emotionally depleted after interacting with them.

Most people that drain us are not conscious of what they do. Whether they want it or do it unconsciously, some individuals are adept at influencing the thoughts and feelings of others, often without us even realizing it. This can happen through:

Negative Interactions: Engaging with someone who constantly criticizes or belittles us can drain our emotional energy. Over time, these interactions can lead to feelings of inadequacy and despair.

Gaslighting: This manipulation tactic involves making someone doubt their perceptions or feelings. It can leave the victim feeling confused and vulnerable, ultimately sapping their emotional strength.

Emotional Contagion: Emotions can be contagious. Being around someone who is chronically negative can affect our mood and energy levels, making us more susceptible to their emotional state.

Even if it's not the above examples who drain our energy, negativity, and criticism can also create a toxic environment and overly dependent relationships can drain our emotional resources by asking for constant support but never offering support in return creating an imbalanced dynamic. Drama and crisis of others that demand time and energy from us and the indirect hostility game of passive and aggressiveness are unhealthy situations to be in also. Protection of the above will be discussed later.

The relationship with a psychic or emotional vampire is characterized by:

• One-sided interactions, where you feel like you are constantly giving but receiving little in return.

• Emotional manipulation or guilt-tripping that keeps you tied to the person, feeling responsible for their well-being.

• A sense of energy depletion, especially after spending time with the individual.

Psychic vampires may or may not intentionally harm you, they might be dealing with their own emotional wounds or lack of self-awareness, but their presence in your life can be highly draining. The cords attached to psychic vampires typically latch onto the solar plexus (personal power) or heart chakra, where they feed on your energy.

The cords that tie you with psychic vampires can be cut by first recognizing the unhealthy nature of the attachment. Setting energetic boundaries is crucial and part of this is cutting cords through visualization, limiting interactions with the person, or completely distancing yourself if necessary. Visualization techniques such as shielding (enveloping yourself in protective light) can also help protect you from further energy drain. A basic example of an active visualization on the subject is the next one.

Psychic Vampire Shielding Visualization

For psychic vampires, focus on protecting your energy first. Visualize a sphere of light (golden or white) surrounding you, forming a protective shield that prevents any further energy drain. Next, identify the cords attached to your solar plexus or heart chakra, and imagine cutting these cords with a sword of light, allowing the energy to be returned to the other person and yourself. Follow up by visualizing your energy field being cleansed and restored with bright, healing light.

The Trap of Attachment: Clinging to What No Longer Serves Us

The trap of attachment refers to the tendency to cling to people, situations, or emotions, even when they no longer serve our growth or well-being. Attachments, in themselves, are natural. We form them with loved ones, friends, and even life experiences. However, when these attachments become toxic or limiting, they can form strong energetic cords that prevent us from evolving and drain our energy.

Attachments may keep us tied to:

• Old relationships, even after they've ended or become dysfunctional.

• Fear-based patterns, such as anxiety, jealousy, or insecurity, which are often rooted in past experiences or trauma.

• Unfulfilled desires or fantasies about how things "should" be, rather than accepting reality as it is.

These cords are often attached to the heart chakra (emotional attachment), the third eye chakra (vision and perception), and sometimes the root chakra (sense of security). The trap of attachment can lead to feelings of dependence, fear of change, or reluctance to move forward.

To break free from the trap of attachment is essential to cultivate detachment, the ability to love or appreciate people and experiences without clinging to them. Practices like mindfulness meditation, acceptance, and forgiveness can help dissolve the cords that tether you to unhelpful attachments. In visualization meditations, like the ones I suggest in this book, you can picture these cords being gently untied or dissolved into light, symbolizing the release of emotional or mental attachment. One basic visualization on attachment release is as follows.

Detachment Meditation for Attachments

To release attachments, begin by sitting in a meditative state and bringing awareness to the people, situations, or emotions that you feel tied to. Visualize the cords extending from your heart or third eye to these attachments. Imagine gently untangling these cords, slowly dissolving them with soft, loving light. As you release the attachment, repeat: "I release what no longer serves me with love and compassion." Feel the release of emotional tension as you free yourself from the burden of attachment.

But what can we do more to stabilize our freedom from these burdens and what is cord-cutting beyond the basics?

What is Cord-Cutting?

Energetic cord-cutting is a powerful tool that allows us to reclaim our energy, restore balance, and protect our emotional well-being. Whether you're dealing with the lingering effects of the past, energy-draining relationships, or unhealthy attachments, releasing these cords gives you the freedom to live with greater clarity, emotional strength, and inner peace.

When you actively engage in cord-cutting practices, you affirm your right to energy sovereignty, the ability to control and protect your own energy. This sense of empowerment helps you maintain healthier, more fulfilling relationships while letting go of anything that drains or diminishes your life force.

There are various practices to clear or cut energetic cords. Some of them include some form of ritual or healing as our mind understands procedures like rituals and every change needs a kind of healing to smooth the past and engage the future. Suggestions are:

1. Cord-Cutting Meditations

Meditative practices where you visualize the cord and consciously cut it, either using imagined scissors or light, can be powerful. These meditations allow you to set the intention to release the cord and restore your energetic autonomy.

2. Energy Healing Practices

Healing modalities like Reiki, chakra balancing, or working with a trained energy healer can help identify and release cords, particularly those that are deeply rooted or unconscious. Energy work helps realign your energy field and remove lingering attachments.

3. Rituals and Affirmations

Using rituals that involve visualization, crystals, candles, or affirmations can support the cord-cutting process. Setting clear intentions and affirming your desire to release any attachments that drain your energy can create powerful shifts.

4. Emotional Healing and Forgiveness

Healing the emotional wounds that created the cords in the first place is one of the most effective ways to release them naturally. By practicing forgiveness, both for others and yourself, and addressing unresolved emotions, the energetic cord dissolves naturally as its emotional charge weakens.

We all have relationships that impact us deeply, some positively while others more negatively. When a relationship ends but continues to drain you, drag you down, or make it impossible to move forward, a practice known as energetic cord-cutting can be a powerful tool for healing and letting go.

A cord-cutting ritual draws from psychological insights and spiritual wisdom and aims to address the lingering emotional attachments that hinder personal growth. It is NOT for petty arguments, everyday disagreements, revenge, or teenage drama. It should be reserved for relationships that are harming you mentally, physically, or spiritually as these are the times when a cord-cutting ceremony can be beneficial to you. Sometimes those cords are strong, and we can't get through it all the first time and that is ok, you're allowed to do it more than once. In fact, traditional cord-cutting has to be done for nine consecutive days around the same time, and losing one day the individual would have to start the practice from day one. But that is not always necessary. The practitioner will know when one ritual is enough or the cords are so strong that need the full 9-day circle to dissolve.

When the cords are especially strong, you can have

- Feelings of general leathery, depression, and unexplained sadness

- Feelings of being 'stuck' or unable to make decisions

- Obsessive thoughts about another person

- Lowered immune function, getting sick often

- Unhealthy habits and addictive behaviors, seeking comfort in excesses such as smoking, binge eating, drinking, drugs, and even seemingly healthy habits such as over-exercising

A cord-cutting ceremony or ritual can be emotional to do. This might be about a person that you have invested years and years of time and emotions with. It could be a family member, spouse, lover, or long-time friend and baby steps are ok. Just make sure to do it when you're ready, and feel safe and you can truly let go. We don't want to do this ritual during a heated moment of anger or rage, it's best to choose this ritual when you are feeling emotionally stable. Cord cutting will help you to move on with your life, and it encourages them to move on with theirs too.

Spiritually cord-cutting involves severing emotional ties that no longer serve our well-being and personal growth. It releases old energy that holds us back, allowing us to heal from past relationships and move forward.

Psychologically it might be seen as a form of emotional detachment or boundary-setting where we consciously decide to cut emotional ties or reduce the impact of a previous relationship on our current emotional state.

We can think of performing cord-cutting when a relationship has ended and you have difficulty moving forward, when you feel particularly drained by an individual and you need to regain your energy and emotional balance, when you are ready to move on but constantly think of a past event or experience or when you are unable to let go of feelings of bitterness or resentment towards someone.

By recognizing, managing, and releasing energetic cords, we can maintain energetic health, reclaim personal power, and cultivate deeper emotional freedom in our lives. After resolving whatever holds us back, we will need to protect our energy and set boundaries valuable and necessary for emotional and energetic well-being.

Cleaning, Protecting and Relaxing

for Ritual

Any energetic or spiritual practice is good to happen in a prepared area that would minimize distraction and is free of negativity. Preparation for the ritual includes both physical and energy cleaning. A place in a mess is not the best place to relax and tidying is good not only for the space but also for the mind that stays undisturbed and easy to relax.

Beyond the peace of mind, any dirty area carries negativity, especially at the corners. It's not that something there is intentionally going to harm you but negativity has the habit of becoming stagnant and its low vibrations undermine the result of the spiritual practice we are going to do.

After physical cleaning and tidying, incense with frankincense, myrrh, sandalwood, or sage. Start from the north corner of the room moving counterclockwise from wall to wall using a sign or a symbol that is sacred to you and symbolizes protection. Imagine a white light spreading where the smoke goes cleaning energetically whatever touches.

Protecting your place is not only to keep negativity outside, something that can affect the quality of your visualization, but it is mostly to give you a sense of security and isolation. It is good to feel that you are safe and also outside of the world beyond this room and you are about to enter another place that is not compatible with your everyday life. You will leave your stress, worries, and everyday thoughts behind.

If other people are in the house, ask them not to disturb you until you finish. Don't forget to visit the bathroom before you start so your body will not need to bring you back. If, for any reason, you will need to leave the area before finishing the visualization, you should keep in mind that you are to come back using the reverse steps of the procedure. If you just completed the protection inside visualization and broke it, know that you should do it again. If you return without taking the steps backwards, your subconscious will be disoriented for some time. No worries, just let yourself some time to rest.

Wear loose clothing that allows you to feel comfortable and will not let you get cold or warm. Light a candle to create atmosphere, and turn off or dim the lights of the room. Sit comfortably in a chair with a back and follow the instructions. You should be comfortable enough to go on with your journey without distractions but not too comfortable so you may sleep.

We start every practice by relaxing body and mind. If they are troubled, you are not able to concentrate on what you are going to do. Or concentration will be of poor quality and you won't go deep enough in your subconscious to have a real experience.

Relaxation is the state of a body that is not in conflict. Our stressful lives made us believe that being stressed all the time is almost natural and we may not believe we can live in harmony with our body anymore. The development of the ability to live relaxed can improve our lives though. An hour of deep relaxation can rest our bodies like the sleep of many hours. A relaxed person doesn't waste energy unconsciously holding the muscles tight for no reason only because of habit.

Body relaxation is a gift to ourselves. It lowers blood pressure, heart rate, and anxiety, relaxes muscle groups, and calms breathing. A calm body has more energy because it is not leaking all the time, helps with concentration since it doesn't interfere with the mind, has greater pain tolerance if need be, and a greater self-healing capacity.

When the body is relaxed, it is much easier to relax the mind. The mind works in specific ways. It can be a secretary and it can be a tool for manifestation. It is usually a confused set of voices, each trying to be on top of the others. In this practice, we will not try to quiet these voices. It is of great difficulty and the aim of another kind of meditation.

Here, we will relax the body and the mind and guide the attention through the different visual images of our journey within. It is easy to step out of the flow, especially when someone is new to meditation. But we will grab our attention and come back. The mind will always want to flee because it is how it is used to. It is not trained to concentrate and focus. We will bring it back and go on with the visualization till the end of it. In time, this will get easier.

After guided meditation is over, it is good to sit for a couple of minutes to let the body absorb the experience. It is ok if you don't manage the perfect meditation the first time. We usually need to try some times to have a result.

Don't forget to read the preparation and the guided meditation enough times to remember all the steps. If you don't want to stress yourself trying to remember and lose the joy of the experience or are afraid you will forget steps in the process, read the text, record it, and play it to guide you.

Clean, protect, and light a candle. Dim or turn off the lights and relax in loose clothes in your chair. You know you are safe in your room during the meditation. You can start keeping a diary of your experiences. Enjoy the journey.

Guided Meditations to Cut the Cords

Sit in your chair with your feet parallel to each other and the soles touching the floor. The back is straight and your head leans gently forward. Your hands rest on the thighs with the palms facing up. Close your eyes. Ask for help, and protection from your guides, the divine being you believe in or the Universe. Let yourself feel comfortable in this position and breathe slowly. Let yourself be. Exhale and inhale slowly from the abdomen letting the air enter your body, go to the different parts, and then leave exhaling. Inhale again slowly and imagine the air entering from the nose as a white cloud that travels through the body, and gets gray from the dirt that collects and goes out of the mouth. Do this once or twice more and feel comfortable.

See with your inner eyes the room where you are. Imagine the objects that exist inside the area. The air seems gray and blurry. You know it's some kind of negativity. Turn your attention to the chakra of your heart, on your spine near your physical heart. It looks like a beautiful green flower with twelve petals. A green aura is swirling around it, sending you waves of love. Feel the love of the heart chakra.

Inhale visualizing a white bright ball of light at the center of the heart chakra. It gets bigger and bigger and slowly fills the chest. Now the white light expands out of you and spreads itself to all directions in the room. While expanding, it touches the negativity that colors gray the internal of the room. The light dissolves all grayness and moves around to create a big white circle with your heart chakra as the center. The circle gets bigger and covers all the room. It is clean and bright. Feel the soothing vibration. The energy stops at the walls. It creates a barrier around the room covering the walls, the floor, and the ceiling. Then, it stabilizes itself as a cocoon. You see it vibrating as alive and know that you are completely safe. The bright light slowly and softly fades away as an image but you know that the cocoon is still there to protect you.

Your body and your mind have started to relax. Imagine now a golden cloud above you. It is bright with a brilliant golden aura around it. Feel its power, strong and tranquil. Suddenly, a golden drop falls on you and then another one. Each drop relaxes the place it touches. The cloud starts to rain. The golden liquid wets your head, clearing and calming your thoughts, and moves down your throat, chest, and hands. Your body becomes golden and bright. Every cell sinks into a deep relaxation. The rain reaches the floor and leaves from there and from the soles of your feet to the earth. Soon, it stops and the cloud disappears. Your body and mind are relaxed and it is time for the main ritual of cord-cutting.

Concentrate your attention inside your head, between your eyebrows, where your third eye is located. You are inside your head behind your third eye and there is a door in front of you where the third eye is. It may be a simple or decorated door, it may be a normal or a square or a round door, or anything that looks like a door. It can be made from steel, wood, or any other material. The important is that this door separates you from a secure place where you can work.

Clear your mind, open the door, and go to the other side.

Look around. You are in a place where your subconscious knows that you feel safe. It may be a forest, a house, or a place next to a river but the most important is that it is familiar to you. Visualize yourself as your spiritual or etheric body with an aura like a bubble of light surrounding you.

Sit down so you are stable and in contact with the earth. Take your time to check your body for long rope-like cords attached to different areas of your body. You may see cords attached to your solar plexus, your heart, your mind, or some other place of your body. They may look like the umbilical cord that connects a mother with her child. They can be of different thicknesses from a small rope to the trunk of a tree. According to its thickness, the cord drains more or less of your energy.

Feel the cords that attracted you most to work with or ask to show you the cord that feels it connects you with the person or the situation that you want to resolve. Where is it attached on your body? It may be one of the thick ones since it drains a lot of your energy. See what it looks like. Is it strong or decaying? How does it feel? Now follow the cord to see what or who it connects you with. It may connect you to a memory that created the situation that drains you or it may lead you to the person taking your energy. See who this person is and check this individual's aura. Is it strong or damaged? Where is the cord connected to this person's body?

Touch the cord and let yourself feel. Do you feel guilty or sad or injured? Do memories or images come to you that are the reasons for your emotions? Let yourself feel the situation while you get a full realization of the relation that created the cord. Sometimes we realize that the person was consciously hurting us or that this is the way this individual does to everyone around or has problems that don't let him or her realize the wrongdoing. We may even get a more objective idea of the situation, which may help us disconnect ourselves from it. Now that you know the who and the how, you are ready to cut the cord.

See your body and the cord attached to it again. Hold it with one hand and prepare to cut with the other. Cutting the cord can be a personal matter. You can use your hand, a knife, even a cleaver or an axe if it is very big, or any other way or object you think suits the occasion. The cord must be cut completely. Sometimes it may feel that it doesn't want to be cut like it is alive or emotional stuff comes up. You cut the cord completely and let it leave away from you even if the cord ends may try to reconnect. Look now at the area where your part of the cord is still attached to your body. It slowly dissolves and shrinks and you imagine it cut from your body. Let it on the ground and imagine it catching fire and burning completely until it is no more. The area where it was attached may be like it is injured or like a wound. Imagine a clear green energy coming from your heart and going there. It is soothing, comforting, and healing this wound. Let the green energy have the time it needs to do the healing and feel the freedom that comes from the cord-cutting. The energy of the heart heals with love and compassion both the wound and yourself removing any residual energies associated with the past emotional attachment. When healed, you can visualize smudging the area with sage to purify your energy as a whole.

Stay at this place in your subconscious as much as you feel like enjoying the new feeling of freedom. You feel energized and rejuvenated. Now, stand up and go back to the door of your third eye. Open it and step in your head behind the third eye chakra. Close the door. Thank your guides, the divine being you believe in, or the Universe for their help and protection.

You are back in your body. Give time to yourself and your body to realize what happened during the guided meditation. Move your hands and slowly open your eyes. Write your experience in the diary of your meditations. Now you can leave the place, drink some water, eat some food, and meet people to ground yourself in your everyday reality.

You can do cord-cutting again when you feel that you need to do so to clear yourself from the other cords that may drain your energy. Work on them to see which are harmful and which you want to keep as they connect you with loved ones. Doing cord-cutting every month is good for your energetic hygiene as we keep creating new cords and some of them are not helpful for our emotional and energetic state.

This was a basic guided meditation for cord-cutting. You can use it as it is or you can adjust it according to what suits you best. Some examples that can give you as alternatives are below.

1. Golden Light Cord-Cutting Meditation

This technique uses the healing power of **golden light** to sever and dissolve energetic cords. It's a gentle yet effective practice for releasing cords and healing your energy field.

"Sit comfortably with your spine straight and feet grounded. Close your eyes and take several deep breaths, allowing yourself to relax. Visualize a brilliant golden light surrounding you, acting as a protective shield. This light is warm, healing, and filled with love.

Close your eyes and picture any energetic cords connected to your body. These cords may be attached to specific areas such as your heart, solar plexus, or throat. Take a moment to identify where you feel the strongest attachment.

Once you've identified the cords, visualize a pair of golden scissors or a golden sword in your hand. Use this tool to cut through each cord gently. As you cut, imagine the cords dissolving into golden light and being absorbed by the Earth for healing and transmutation.

After the cords are cut, visualize the golden light filling in the spaces where the cords were attached, healing any energy imbalances and sealing your energy field.

Take a deep breath, feeling yourself fully grounded in your body, free from any unwanted attachments. When you're ready, open your eyes and return to the present moment, carrying a sense of peace, freedom, and clarity with you."

2. Forgiveness Cord-Cutting Visualization

This technique combines **forgiveness** with cord-cutting, allowing you to release the emotional charge behind the cords, particularly in difficult or strained relationships.

Konstantia Karletsa

"Sit comfortably in a quiet space, close your eyes, and take a few deep breaths to center yourself. Bring to mind the person or situation you wish to release. Visualize them standing or sitting in front of you. In your mind, say to the person: **"I forgive you, and I release you. I forgive myself, and I release myself."** You may add any words of forgiveness or healing that feel right for you.

As you speak these words, visualize a cord of light connecting you to the person or situation. With each breath, the cord becomes more visible. Imagine a soft, glowing light surrounding you, radiating from your heart. Hold in your hand a pair of sharp, glowing scissors or a blade of light.

Gently cut through the cord, severing the energetic tie between you and the person or situation. As you cut, say mentally or out loud: **"I release you with love and peace."** Watch as the cord falls away and dissolves into light. Feel the space where the cord was attached being filled with love and healing energy.

Take a moment to breathe deeply and feel the sense of freedom and emotional release. You may wish to mentally thank the person for any lessons learned, as this completes the process of letting go with love."

3. Full Body Cord-Cutting Meditation

This meditation is a full-body scan designed to identify and cut multiple energetic cords at once. It helps clear your energy field after emotional stress, a difficult breakup, or a major life change.

"Find a quiet, comfortable place to sit or lie down. Close your eyes and focus on your breath, inhaling and exhaling deeply. Begin by visualizing a large ball of white or golden light above your head. This light represents pure, divine energy, ready to cleanse and heal.

Slowly move the ball of light down over your body, starting at the crown of your head. As it moves, it highlights any cords attached to your energy field. These cords may appear as dark threads, ropes, or energetic attachments. As the light scans over each cord, visualize it shining brighter and cutting through the cord, dissolving it completely. Imagine each cord being absorbed by the Earth for healing.

Continue scanning your body, moving from your head down through your neck, shoulders, arms, chest, abdomen, legs, and feet, cutting any cords you find along the way. Once you've scanned your entire body, visualize the white or golden light expanding around you, creating a protective, healing bubble that seals and protects your energy field from future attachments.

Sit quietly for a few moments, breathing deeply and feeling fully cleansed, grounded, and free from any unwanted energetic connections."

4. Chakra Cord-Cutting Visualization

Energetic cords often attach themselves to different **chakras** (energy centers in the body). This method focuses on clearing cords from specific chakras that may be holding onto past energy or emotions.

"Sit in a meditative posture, close your eyes, and take a few calming breaths.

Starting at your **root chakra** (located at the base of your spine), imagine a bright red light spinning in this area. Visualize any cords attached to this chakra, particularly those tied to security, safety, or past trauma. Imagine gently cutting these cords with a blade or scissors made of light.

Move up to your **sacral chakra** (lower abdomen), visualizing a bright orange light. Cut any cords attached here that may be connected to relationships, creativity, or emotional wounds.

Continue moving upward through each chakra—**solar plexus** (yellow, self-esteem), **heart chakra** (green, love and relationships), **throat chakra** (blue, communication), **third eye** (indigo, intuition), and **crown chakra** (violet, spiritual connection)—repeating the process of visualizing cords and cutting them.

After you've cleared cords from all seven chakras, imagine a stream of white light flowing from the top of your head to the base of your spine, sealing your energy centers and balancing your energy."

The Aftermaths of Cord-Cutting

Cord-cutting rituals help individuals achieve closure from past relationships, particularly those that have left lasting emotional wounds. However, it can also lead to temporary feelings of emptiness or disorientation as one adjusts to the absence of familiar energies.

The key benefits of a cord-cutting ritual are:

- *Achieving closure from past relationships*: The act of cord-cutting can provide a sense of finality and closure to past relationships that may still be causing emotional distress.

- *Healing emotional wounds*: By severing the energetic cords tied to painful memories or experiences, the ritual can facilitate healing and recovery from those emotional wounds.

- *Freeing up energy for personal development*: Energetic cords can drain energy. By cutting them, you free up this energy to be used for your personal growth and development.

- *Promoting emotional growth*: The practice of cord-cutting provides a symbolic act of releasing past resentment, regret, or bitterness — enabling you to let go of any emotional baggage and better respond to future emotional experiences.

- Facilitating a shift towards positivity: By severing ties with past negative experiences, you can welcome an energetic shift, paving the way for positivity and growth in your life.

It's important to approach cord-cutting with compassion for yourself and others. The process is not about anger or rejection but about freeing yourself from energetic ties that may be holding you back. Once the cords are cut, you can move forward with a renewed sense of peace, autonomy, and emotional freedom.

The effectiveness of a cord-cutting ritual relies on patience and often requires multiple attempts. Success in severing emotional ties and fostering personal healing may take time, necessitating repeated efforts. Patience is crucial as individuals navigate the complexities of their emotional landscapes, unveiling layers of attachment. The iterative nature underscores the depth of the healing journey, emphasizing that transformative effects unfold gradually through dedication.

After completing a cord-cutting meditation or visualization, it's essential to ground yourself and replenish your energy. Cord-cutting can leave you feeling lighter but also a bit raw or ungrounded. Ground and restore your energy as below:

- Grounding Exercises: After cutting cords, you may want to engage in a grounding practice such as walking barefoot on the Earth, doing deep breathing exercises, or visualizing roots growing from your feet into the Earth. This helps you reconnect with your body and the present moment.

- Energy Cleansing: Consider using tools like smudging (with sage, myrrh, or another cleansing herb), taking a salt bath (sea salt or Epsom salt works well), or surrounding yourself with healing crystals (such as black tourmaline for protection, selenite for clearing, or amethyst for spiritual connection). These methods help clear residual energy and support your body in healing after the cord-cutting process.

- Affirmations and Intentions: To reinforce your emotional and energetic shift, you may wish to say affirmations like, "I release what no longer serves me," or "I reclaim my energy and welcome healing into my life." Setting a clear intention for your future growth helps solidify the release of past attachments.

- Rest and Self-Care: Cord-cutting can be emotionally intense, so allow yourself time to rest, recover, and reflect. Self-care activities like meditation, journaling, or simply relaxing can help you integrate the effects of the cord-cutting session and restore your energy balance.

Signs that your cord-cutting practice is working, include

- Having a profound sense of freedom
- Feeling unburdened and liberated

- A sense that considerable weight has been lifted off your shoulders

You might also experience a surge in energy. This increased vitality indicates you're successfully severing the negative ties depleting your energy reserves.

Another common indication that your cord-cutting technique is working is a reduced emotional reaction to thoughts about a specific person or situation. You might find you can maintain a more balanced and detached perspective rather than feeling overwhelmed by emotions when thinking about them.

How does cord-cutting affect the other person? The focus of cord-cutting is on self-improvement and finding inner peace. It is an internal process — changing your energy without attempting to alter others' perceptions of you.

While the primary objective of cord-cutting is focused on one's internal energy and well-being, it's important to recognize that this practice can inadvertently impact the other person's energy since he or she stops feeling empowered with your energy. This acknowledgment underscores the interconnected nature of relationships.

The effects of cord-cutting may extend beyond the emotional realm and manifest in both physical and mental aspects.

Physically, cord-cutting may result in a reduced sense of stress and tension in interactions with the individual for both you and the other person.

Mentally, it can contribute to a more balanced and detached perspective, promoting a healthier dynamic for both of you.

Imagine yourself now being cloaked in a luminescent blanket of energetic protection. This coating of light is your energetic boundary. See and feel how this boundary helps you to maintain your highest level of energy. Intend that this boundary remains in place as you step confidently forward into your life.

What Do We Do Next

So, we have done the cord-cutting meditation and we know now the results of it. We have a feeling of energy and freedom we didn't have for a long time. What do we need to do to protect ourselves from now on?

To take your energy back and keep it, it would be good to protect it using

Self-Awareness: Cultivating self-awareness is crucial. Recognizing your thoughts and feelings allows you to identify patterns and triggers. Journaling or mindfulness practices can help enhance this awareness.

Setting Clear Boundaries: It's essential to establish boundaries with individuals who drain your energy. This could mean limiting your time with them or learning to say no.

Communicate Openly: If someone is consistently draining your energy, consider discussing your feelings with them. Sometimes, they may not realize their impact.

Positive Relationships: Surround yourself with supportive, positive people. Engaging with those who uplift you can help counteract negative influences.

Emotional Self-Care: Practice self-care activities that nurture your emotional well-being, such as exercise, hobbies, and spending time in nature. These activities can replenish your energy and strengthen your resilience.

Understanding the interplay between thoughts, feelings, and external influences is vital for maintaining emotional health. By becoming more aware of how these elements work, we can take proactive steps to protect our energy and foster a more positive mindset. This awareness allows us to build healthier relationships and create an environment that supports our growth and well-being. Another way of restoring energy and enhancing wellness is grounding.

The Importance of Grounding

Grounding, also known as earthing, is a practice that helps reconnect us to the Earth's energy and brings our awareness into the present moment. It involves techniques that stabilize and balance our emotional, physical, and spiritual energy. Grounding is essential for those who feel overwhelmed, anxious, or disconnected from their bodies, as it helps restore a sense of calm, clarity, and inner peace.

In our daily lives, we often get "caught up" in our thoughts, stress, or external situations, which can cause us to feel unbalanced, scattered, or emotionally drained. Grounding brings our focus back to the here and now, anchoring us in our body and the present moment.

It is a technique that help us recover from a cord-cutting ritual or visualization even when we think we don't need it. It will balance our energies and give us a new perspective in life.

Grounding has many benefits for overall well-being:

- **Reduces anxiety and stress**: Grounding can help calm the nervous system by bringing attention back to the body, and reducing racing thoughts and worries.

- **Enhances mental clarity**: By grounding, you can clear mental fog and enhance focus, which allows for better decision-making and mindfulness.
- **Rebalances energy**: When we feel emotionally drained or scattered, grounding helps stabilize our energy, allowing us to regain balance and be in the moment.
- **Physical benefits**: Grounding can have a direct effect on the body, including improved sleep, reduced inflammation, and a sense of overall relaxation.

Grounding works by drawing your awareness back to your body and the Earth. The Earth's energy is naturally stabilizing, and by making contact with it—either through physical means or visualization—you can discharge excess energy (like stress, anxiety, or overwhelm) and restore a balanced state.

In metaphysical terms, grounding connects you to the Earth's energy field, helping to realign your energetic body. From a psychological standpoint, grounding exercises bring you into a mindful state, breaking the cycle of stress or rumination and helping you feel more centered.

Grounding can be practiced in a variety of ways. Here are several effective grounding exercises to help you regain balance:

1. Barefoot Walking on the Earth

One of the simplest and most effective grounding techniques is walking barefoot on natural surfaces like grass, dirt, sand, or even stone. This allows direct contact with the Earth's electromagnetic field, which can help reset your energy.

- Find a natural environment like a park, garden, or beach.
- Remove your shoes and socks and walk barefoot on the ground.
- As you walk, focus on the sensation of your feet touching the Earth. Feel the texture of the ground beneath you and notice how it feels on your skin.
- Imagine energy flowing from the Earth into your body through your feet, helping you feel more anchored and stable.

You can do this for 5–15 minutes to feel more connected and grounded.

2. Tree Visualization Grounding

If you're unable to physically connect with the Earth, this visualization exercise helps you create a grounding connection through imagery. This practice is great for when you're indoors or need a quick grounding reset.

- Sit or stand in a comfortable position, close your eyes, and take a few deep breaths.
- Imagine that you are a tree. Visualize your feet or the base of your spine growing roots that extend deep into the Earth.
- Picture these roots digging into the soil, going deeper and deeper until they reach the Earth's core. Imagine drawing energy from the Earth through your roots and into your body.
- Feel the Earth's energy rise through your legs, grounding you and bringing stability to your body and mind.
- You can stay in this visualization for a few minutes, breathing deeply and feeling connected to the Earth's nourishing energy.

3. The 5-4-3-2-1 Grounding Technique (Sensory Grounding)

This exercise helps you ground by engaging your senses and bringing you back to the present moment. It's especially effective for reducing anxiety or panic attacks.

- Look around and identify 5 things you can **see**.

- Next, close your eyes and identify 4 things you can **feel** (for example, the texture of your clothes, the chair you're sitting on, the ground under your feet).
- Then, focus on 3 things you can **hear** (the hum of a fan, birds chirping, distant voices).
- Identify 2 things you can **smell** (this could be the scent of your skin, the air, or something nearby).
- Finally, identify 1 thing you can **taste** (if nothing comes to mind, imagine a taste like fresh mint or chocolate).

This exercise immediately draws your focus to your surroundings, pulling you out of your head and into the present moment.

4. Body Scan Meditation

This grounding technique focuses on bringing awareness to different parts of the body, releasing tension, and helping you reconnect with your physical self.

- Sit or lie down in a comfortable position. Close your eyes and take a few deep, slow breaths.
- Start by focusing on your toes. Notice any sensations—whether it's warmth, tingling, or tension—and simply observe.
- Gradually move your awareness upward through your feet, ankles, calves, knees, thighs, hips, and

so on, all the way to your head. As you scan each part of your body, allow any tension to release.

- With each exhale, imagine tension and stress leaving your body, while with each inhale, imagine a sense of grounding and relaxation spreading through you.

This exercise helps calm both your mind and body, bringing you into a more grounded and present state.

5. Grounding with Breathwork

Breathwork is a powerful tool for grounding. Conscious breathing helps bring awareness to the body and quiets the mind, making it a great practice for restoring balance and focus.

- Sit comfortably with your feet flat on the ground and your spine straight.
- Take a deep breath in for a count of 4, hold for 4, and then exhale for a count of 6.
- As you exhale, imagine that any stress or excess energy is being released down into the Earth through your feet.
- With each inhale, imagine drawing in calm, grounding energy from the Earth. Feel it rise up

through your legs, filling your body with a sense of stability and peace.

- Continue this breathing pattern for 5–10 minutes or until you feel more centered.

6. Holding a Grounding Object like a Crystal

Some people find that holding a specific object helps anchor their energy. This could be a crystal, rock, or any personal item that feels grounding to you.

- Choose an object that feels solid and calming in your hand, such as a smooth stone, crystal (like hematite or black tourmaline), or another meaningful item.
- Sit quietly and hold the object in your hand. Focus on its texture, temperature, and weight.
- Allow yourself to become absorbed in the sensation of holding it, feeling your energy stabilize and ground as you focus on the object.

This can be done anywhere, and it's especially useful for those who need a quick grounding reset during the day.

Grounding as a Daily Practice

Incorporating grounding into your daily routine can greatly improve your emotional, mental, and physical well-being.

Whether it's through a mindful walk in nature, a few minutes of grounding breathwork, or a quick sensory exercise, grounding is a valuable tool for managing stress, restoring balance, and maintaining a deeper connection to yourself and the world around you.

By practicing grounding regularly, you create a foundation of stability that supports both your energy and your mental clarity, allowing you to navigate life's challenges with greater ease and presence.

Small Biography of the Author

Konstantia Karletsa was born in Thessaloniki, Greece. Now she lives in Katerini, a city near Olympus, the mountain of the ancient Greek gods. She has two daughters and lives with her husband and four cats that adopted her.

From early years, she was inclined to the strange and the unknown, and she went through many jobs and family situations. She studied and experimented with esoteric paths, especially guided meditation. In 2008, she became vegan because of her love, empathy, and compassion for all creatures.

The result of her work with guided meditation and her love for all animals is a book published in 2017 after many years of research about totem animals. "The Book of Totems" published by Gaiastron Publications was written in Greek, her native language, and has been translated into English and German.

After the success of her book, she was asked and gave seminars on power animals and other esoteric subjects usually connected with guided meditation. During the pandemic, she gave group seminars online. Now she writes new books and paints on a professional basis.

She is the owner of https://konstantiakarletsa.com website, where she exhibits her paintings as a professional painter and her writings. She also hosts the professional test to reveal each person's power animal. It's a 100-question multiple-choice test that you can find at https://konstantiakarletsa.com/power-animal-test/.

Konstantia Karletsa's other books

- The Book of Totems

- Das Buch der Totem

- Meet Your Power Animal

- Find Your Inner Home

Printed in Dunstable, United Kingdom

67319548R00038